The Absolutely Essential Book of Jokes about the Left

PHILIP DUNN

THE CHOIR PRESS

First published in the United Kingdom in 2017 by
The Choir Press

ISBN 978-1-911589-22-8

Contents

Introduction

Question: What do you normally get if you have a Conservative or former Blairite minister and a left-wing comedian appearing jointly on the BBC topical debate programme *Question Time?*

Answer: A government minister who is at a disadvantage because she/he doesn't know any anti-left comedian jokes of course. (Ten months ago I sent some of these to Boris Johnson, Teresa May, Lord Mandelson of Guacamole, and Terence Wright-Clod, Lord Rush of Blighty, and the latter said he'd definitely give them a try.)

In this and similar BBC settings the inevitable leftist, anti-Tory jibes and grand-standing seem to have the edge, and colour public feeling – not just about ministers and policies, but the United Kingdom itself. This is no laughing matter. We are entitled to feel better about Britain and its past. An unprepared patriotic Brit, like Sheffield postmaster Deva Kumarasiri, stands little chance (perhaps) against a lefty stand-up or Marxified social justice warrior, even if we think we have a handle on the left. They will always mock national sentiments and values, and the apprehensions of many about uncontrolled immigration. We too, then, are at a disadvantage at those moments. We lack the advantages of humour and mockery. For too long the left have monopolised these instruments, and sarcasm and insults continue to be part of their modus operandi.

What can we do about this unequal situation? Well, we can turn the tables on the lefty stand-ups for starters – by using jokes, wit, invective, humour, and sarcasm; or, better still, some upcoming, non-left political stand-up might? Information and insights about the left, and the ability to identify leftist language and mores, are also valuable, and the content here provides that too, as does the book's part-irreverent **Glossary.**

It is important that the prevailing left orthodoxy in Britain's cultural institutions is made known and rebuffed, and joke forms have a role to play in achieving that end. The challenge is essential if we are to see left ideology and mockery exposed in all its strands; and the jokes, one-liners, mini-sketches, parodies, and jibes in this book are offered for that purpose – should the reader wish to use them. I am, of course, not urging you to do so.

So, no: don't be a rebel; don't recite mild anti-Marcuse and Foucault jokes to a neo-Marxist lecturer outside the London School of Economics or Columbia University. That is serious; that would be terrible. And you might be charged with a hate crime. Nor is it essential for you to nail, thesis-like, your jokes to the front door of the LSE or the School of Oriental & African Studies. I'm not trying it. (They don't have a wooden door as such. It's all portal now.) It is not essential for you to use these jokes at all. You could always write your own and, hippy-like, turning the tables, tape them to one of the trees outside the SOAS. That will fool the No Platform NUS apparatchiks.

But the political comedy scene in the UK is not absolutely leftist. A few non-lefty, quasi 'alternative' stand-ups have substantial TV and radio credits to their name, and comedy awards. Let us hope Geoff Norcott and Andrew Lawrence might achieve major prominence as alternatives to the smug, left-wing comics on BBC Radio 4's *The News Quiz*. Lawrence was bold enough to comment on such figures in 2014, albeit in a Facebook post. Mocking them in his act might well see him hounded for his pains. There are also a number of Christian stand-ups on the circuit, Andy Kind and Milton Jones having the fuller profiles. Christian and pro-Republican comedians abound in the USA, among them Brad Stine, Chonda Pierce (the 'Queen of Clean'), Dennis Miller, Jay Leno, Drew Carey, and Leslie Norris Townsend.

It would be enough if the reader found this book to be a tonic against leftist propaganda and invective. That it might well simply delight is an added bonus, and that motive, along with the mischievous, figured large in the writing of the material.

~~~~~~~~~~~~~~~~~~~~~

These pages include jokes and lines on neo-Marxism, and on the 'alternative' comedians and artistes of the present, and the Thatcher-years. Many of the latter are still with us. Who are the rebels and who are the conformists now? 'Did you hear the one about Alexei Sayle?' Well, it's in this book.

With things turned on their head then, how fitting it is to recruit Al Murray – yes, as a real pub landlord – to the new cultural vanguard. He's a veritable sage in the book's numerous pub jokes – barring Russell Brand and Derek Hatton, full of bright observations on Nicola Sturgeon and a benighted Ed Miliband. He has a knowledge of the incongruities surrounding radical feminism. If only we could get Al Murray to give up being a genuine pub landlord – at the Bolshie Arms, near LSE – and become the contra-left comedian vanguard, Home Guard, or Home Front even; or just plain Captain. Watch this heterotopia, er, space.

And then there's anarchist humour. Class War

themselves offer unmatched hilarity here. You couldn't script it. Surely it can't be for real, or is it? And what about left intellectualism? Have you considered that a country can become overly intellectualised, that is, Marxified? Well, there's a batch of Critical Theory parrot jokes on that. There are over thirty relating to Jeremy Corbyn and Corbynites, and many on the current Scottish Independence scene.

Who'd have thought that the time-honoured light bulb joke – born in the US – could provide such essential left-lampooning wattage: for the light from Lenin's skull illumines Red Clydeside once again, and Venezuela now has a plan for introducing Capitalist energy efficient light bulbs – but it's not a Cuban or Russian one. To begin the book with light bulb jokes and later resort to candles is not to imply that England's Nationalised grid would fail irretrievably under the 2020 (or 2017) Corbyn Labour government, or that cabinet minister Derek Hatton would definitely be the UK's Buffet Organiser for the Syriza visit in the first month of that government. As with these darkling, (perhaps) unlikely visions, enjoy the other light bulb moments about the left which this book provides.

**How many socialists does it take to change a light bulb?
'The answer is Socialism!'**

Acknowledgements

Philip Dunn is the writer, collector, and compiler of the jokes, lines, verse, and text in this book.

I am grateful to the editor of *The Idler* literary magazine for giving me permission to use an extensive excerpt from the Class War interview, conducted by Tom Hodgkinson, in *The Idler* magazine, Issue 43, 2009: Back to the Land: 'Taking Liberties'.

Every attempt has been made to contact copyright holders and sources. These are stated in brackets where known, but if any have been inadvertently overlooked the author would be glad to hear from them.

I am also grateful to professor Jeremy Black for his editing of the book's substantial glossary.

From Anarchists to Zapatistas

* An anarcha-feminist, a Catholic feminist, a Tory feminist, a SlutWalk feminist, Beyoncé, and Mary Berry walk into a pub together.
  The clued-up pub landlord, the astute Al Murray, says: 'What is this, some kind of joke?'

* How many British Anarchists does it take to write an *Anarchist Greatest Heroes* book? The twenty or so were at it ten years ago, now they're down to two, Anarchism is commodified by triumphant Capitalism, and they're still arguing.

* How many anarcho-primitivists does it take to change a light bulb? Why should they change it – they deliberately broke the thing in the first place as part of their attempt to destroy the oppressive, technological mega-machine we live under.

* How many anti-civ anarchists does it take to screw in a light bulb?
  '. . . Who says we need light bulbs?!?'

* How many Black Bloc anarchists does it take to change a light bulb? Only one, but it takes twenty others to film it.

* Why did the Pirate Party member cross the road? To avoid the Anarchist who'd harangue him for appropriating black for his flag and combining it with a diagonal of orange.

* What do you get if you cross an inner-city situationist with a Mafioso? A guy who makes you a street artwork you can't refuse, and never asked for, won't like, and can't get rid of. But, hey, there it is.

* What's an insurrecto's favourite physical exercise? Anarchism.

* How many fearless Bristol anarchists does it take to set fire to a Bristol railway station's signalling cables? All twelve, but it takes an heroic Italian anarchist to show them how to be that insurrectionary.

✻ Tom Hodgkinson, interviewer, *The Idler*, literary and philosophical magazine, 'Taking Liberties', 2009:

TH: *Now most people think of Anarchy as violent and aggressive. But to me it is all about voluntary action and independence. [...] What's your idea of liberty, anarchy, freedom?*

Ian Bone [publisher of Class War]: Pretty much the same as yours: a world without work, a world of unlicensed pleasure. I certainly don't go for that right-to-work bollocks. [...]

TH: *How have things changed since you two first came to London thirty or forty years ago?*

Ray Roughler-Jones [author of poem 'Kill A Tory']: *In Wales, signing on for us was a full-time job. The only people I knew who had jobs were people who were just about to have a court appearance. Nowadays, with the questions they ask you before you go on a medical, you can work out all* the conditions to get *on the sick [...] 'bad back' used to be the only clincher [...] now with the Internet you can authoritatively claim to have the symptoms of Ebola virus and they'll sort you out sharpish.*

TH: *And when did you both take against work?*

RRJ: It's just that nobody worked, none of our friends worked.

IB: No one ever worked [. . .] in Bash the Rich [Bone's biography] *there's a story about 'turning to the working class' but we didn't know anyone who was working! We were all on the dole so we started a Claimants' Union, a union for people on the dole. We would fight to get you all your entitlements. The classic line was: 'If they get you a job, we'll fight your case!' There were all the jokes about what occupation you gave when you were signing on: Father Christmas, snow clearer, and so on. One job I gave was 'Coronation Programme Seller'. 'What's that then, Mr Bone?' asked a puzzled clerk. 'Very long hours. On the day, you're up at five in the morning till all hours,' I countered – not mentioning I hadn't had the luck of securing such a position since 1953!*

TH: Is it actually responsible to be claiming dole from the State?

RRJ: Well, the less money they have to start wars.

TH: Is it easier now, or harder?

IB: It's just as easy. My son was sent for a job in Cashbusters in Bristol. How was he going to get out of it? I said, well, first ask about unions. What sort of union is there? Then the clincher – ask about paternity leave.

TH: So you advise your son on how not to work?

IB: Like a duck to water. He just didn't want to take a glorified debt collection job.

TH: Does the skiving thing go back for generations, do you think?

RRJ: It's not exactly skiving. It's hard graft to be on the dole. They never leave you alone [. . .]

* How many Red Brigade members does it take to change a light bulb? Two. One to change it, and the other to compare it to Mussolini.

* How many Red Brigade members does it take to change a light bulb?
'*Avanti* the light bulb smashers!'

* How many English Angry Brigade members does it take to smash a Ministry of Defence light bulb? Steady on.

* How many English Angry Brigade members does it take to smash a Ministry of Defence light bulb? Just the angriest member, but, boy, does he get excited when he hears it pop.

* How many English Angry Brigade members does it take to smash a Ministry of Defence light bulb? Ultimately, all thirty-six: one angry one to smash it, and thirty-five who attend just for the excitement of hearing it pop.

* Why do people take an instant dislike to socialists? To save time later.

* How many Socialist Workers Party members does it take to change a light bulb? Four. One to change the bulb, one to write about it for 'the paper', one to sell you 'the paper', and another to follow you home and ask you why you weren't at the bulb changing, if you plan to make the next one, and if you are still committed.

* How many Militant Tendency activists does it take to screw in a light bulb? The answer is Socialism.

* Socialism can only arrive by bicycle. (Jose Antonio Viera-Gallo)

* Communism can only arrive by tank.

* How many socialists does it take to change a light bulb? Two. One to screw it in and a second to hand out leaflets.

* How many Occupiers does it take to change a light bulb? I don't know – we're still looking for consensus on if the room is dark, but we're putting together a light-bulb-changing working group and we anticipate a detailed press release sometime over the next week.

* How many lefties does it take to change a light bulb? None, they just sit in the dark and blame Thatcher.

* How many environmentalists does it take to change a light bulb?
Not applicable. LED lights last longer than environmentalists. (While I knew LED had a long life span, I hadn't realised how long. How long will these LED lights last? At 100,000 hours, a light on for 3 hours a day will last 91 years. At 8 hours a day it will last 34 years. At 12 hours a day will last 22 years, and if you run it continuously for 24 hours a day it will last 11 years. Given that the average light is only on for 3 hours a day, the next time you replace your lights bulbs with LED could be your last time.)

* How many Rag Week students can you cram into a socialist's Mitsubishi 4WD?
'Well, five at most, as mine has only got five seats, and they'd have to have clean feet.'

* How many SWP/Scot Nat 'numpties' does it take to change a light bulb? None, they just sit in the dark and blame Capitalism, and the English.

* How many Radical Independence Campaign conference delegates changed one light bulb in Glasgow Auditorium? All three thousand, such was the surge of empowerment and show of solidarity.

* Nicola Sturgeon walks into a Glasgow South Side pub and proceeds to chat with the regulars at some length. The astute Al McMurray, the pub landlord, says: 'What's this? Am I witness to a revolutionary act?'

* What do the initials WRP stand for? Worked-up Revolutionary Party.

* How many Forum Members does it take to change a light bulb? Seventeen Green standards forum zealots to point out that light bulbs have been deprecated in the LB 2.1 spec, and one to call upon everybody to ignore this deprecation.

* How many neo-Zapatistas does it take to replace a Capitalist light bulb? Three: one to change it, one to formally hail the new Capitalist light bulb 'All-Illuminating-Subcomandante Marcos', and Naomi Klein, cultural attaché, to extol the ritual.

Individuals & fun revolutionaries

* Billy Bragg walks into his local pub in Burton Bradstock. He gets his guitar out.
  The barman says: Hi, Bill, nice to see you. 'Lady in Red' would be better than that 'Red Flag' one.

* Buzz-buzz!
  Who's there?
  It's us, Billy, the Dale Farm residents. Can we stay in your grounds?
  Er, sorry, that's not possible.
  Oh, what about Burton Bradstock, then?

* Will Self dies and goes to Heaven? He deliberately arrives early at the pearly gates and proceeds, typically, to give the heavenly citadel the walk-around, idling here and there in his progress as his fancy takes him. He bumps into a purposeful John Bunyan and gives him short shrift. Back late at the gates, he casts a

condescending glance on Saint Peter, the seraphim, and the assembled host, and declares: 'Will Self himself, uncowled: the unpolluted self no less – for your delectation, edification, and *redemption!*' Within weeks he creates pandemonium.

* Russell Brand walks into a pub.
The pub landlord, the cultured Al Murray, says to him: 'You're barred, Chomskyite! Chomskyism, sir, is the last refuge of a scoundrel.'

* Buzz-buzz.
Who is it?
Russell, it's Ed here.
Ed who?
Ed Miliband, Leader of the Labour Party?
Oh, sorry, mate, press the buzzer again and come up.
Thanks, mate, you're a star.

* Knock, knock.
Who's there?
Bea Campbell.
Don't ask me to be calm. What do you want?
I'm conducting an ambitious and wholly impartial survey about Patriarchy in Britain and how it still structures our society today. It involves in total just forty-two correct answers.

❋ Tony Benn always had a silver tongue in his head, and now it's making him a lot of silver. (Dennis Healey)

❋ Did you hear the one about the well-heeled Marxist stand-up and writer Alexei Sayle? He luxuriates in loathing everything so much he has to punch himself in the head when it gets too bad. You could say that it's his ultimate punch line. He is clearly – in Marxist terms – alienated from himself, and Capitalises on it.

❋ What do you get if you cross a cosplay situationist with a Mafioso? A posh young bird who makes you a Pirate Jenny costume you can't refuse.

❋ Oh, look, there's that marvellous Maxine Peake from Luddite Land loudly enunciating again the Romantic poet Shelley: 'GIVE US LIBERTY OR DEATH. RISE LIKE LIONS AFTER SLUMBER!' On the stage backdrop there's a sponsorship notice and logo: Sponsored by NatWest Bank Manchester.

❋ Knock, knock.
Who's there?
George.
George who?
This is George Galloway calling!

* 'Dad, why does that man on the TV not like the London Olympic Games? He's like a monk.'
'Oh dear, him again. He's full of him Self. It's because he's an intellectual, sweetie. Few of them like sport and corporate logos. I think they're a rare breed. Hard to spot them at first.'

* What is the difference between a dead Frankie Boyle in the road and a dead dog? Skid marks in front of the dog.

* How many lefty luvvies does it take to screw in a light bulb? Four or five every general election. Certainly, what comes round goes round, and that light bulb will make a difference. However, viewers are likely to switch off.

* What's woolly and bleats, well-spotted, and red-faced? A dippy sheep named Emma. She wanders off into so many fields, it was likely she'd end up splattered.

* What do you call a left-winger who's an own-goal specialist, and in the wrong position. Gary Lineker. A transfer isn't likely.

* How many hyper-charged nihilist white rap poets does it take to change a light bulb? No need. Just get the electrifying Kate Tempest to exhort it back to life from out its bleak, existential cell.

* Did you hear Tommy Sheridan is going back into politics...? He's forming an Ann Summers Party.

* **Questions to perplex or annoy certain leftists:**

Will Self: Is there any garden centre in Greater London, Will, that you'd recommend as particularly spiritual?

Seamus Milne: If you're interested, Seamus, I know a man who's got two Jack Vettrianos for sale.

Jeremy Hardy: What's your favourite canapés, Jeremy?

Mark Steel: What's your favourite canapés?

Frankie Boyle: They tell me you love canapés.

Susan Calman: What's your favourite Rambo film?

Sandi Toksvig: Have you any more jokes about Nigel Farage's testicular cancer and Hitler?

Rhona Cameron: Are you going to the Black Friday sales this year?

Russell Brand: Have you read Edmund Burke's *Reflections On the Revolution in France?* You must read it.

Marcus Brigstock: Marcus, is it true Laurie Penny discovered that you concealed on your person *Men Are from Mars, Women Are from Venus?*

Stop the War Coalition protestors: Gosh, how did our oil get under their sand?

Irvine Welsh: Hi, baw face, greatest o' Scrots. Guess what, I'm a descendant of Adam Smith, *moral philosopher.* In all Capitalism, Irvine, there is much profit for socialists, and he that resorteth tae penis jokes can rightly add to his fortune, and return to sunny USA. Aye, choose life.

Jane Garvey, presenter of BBC Radio 4 *Woman's Hour:*
Jane, if you want them, I've got an old bar of Sunlight
soap and a washboard in my attic. I think you were
looking for an alternative to Unilever global brand
detergents and scented fabric softeners in supermarkets?
There is no logo on the soap, you'll be pleased to hear.
However, you'll surely know that Lever Brothers
manufactured Sunlight soap.

Emma Thompson: Oh, Emma – Donald Trump: surely,
he's the ultimate 'man in a suit'.

To: Tariq Ali @ Verso Press.
Bcc: Lawrence & Wishart; Pluto Press; Revenge Ink;
Manifesto Press; Dave Spart Press; Cave Press; Tricoteuse
Press; Clenched Fist; Sappho Press; Uncoupling Press;
Avanti Publishing; Blackjack Press; Trickster Press;
Leveller Books; Nightstick Books; Saturnine Publishing;
Banshee Press; Red Clydeside Press; Zap Ink.

Subject: Conference venue in the North: Title: 'Left Publishers – What's Left?'

Dear Tariq, Radical North Conference Venues here regarding your conference, 'Left Publishers –What's Left?'. We have located a Birmingham venue large enough for your stated needs; it is: The Mason's Arms, Bevin Street, Chamberlain Boulevard. For the North of England, there was no venue or public house with the name Gramsci in the title. Do you wish me to book the Mason's Arms room for you?

Ideology: It's damn lonely, and dark

* How many leftists does it take to change a light bulb? Two. One to change it, and the other to compare it to Hitler.

* How many Angry Brigade members does it take to smash one Ministry of Defence light bulb? Actually, the whole thirty-six. They get so excited when they hear it pop.

* How many Foucaultists does it take to change a light bulb?
'No, we must *remove* them all. All power, all enlightenment, must be scrutinised if we are to overcome it.'

* How many Chomskyites does it take to change a light bulb?
'There's no point. It is a Hegemonic light bulb and will therefore implode in good time, as will all the others universally. Such was ancient Athens. Let it come.'

* Is it true that Adam and Eve were the first socialists? Perhaps. Adam and Eve dressed very humbly, had a modest desire for food, and didn't dwell in their own home. But above all, they believed they lived in paradise.

* What do you get when you put four socialists in a room? Five splinter groups.

* How many radical solipsists does it take to change a light bulb? Just one. No one else exists. It's damn lonely and dark being just the one.

* Knock, knock.
  Who's there?
  Bella Caledonia.
  Bella who? An' whit dji want?
  Bella Caledonia here – that we Scots might clasp the Holy Grail. It was Scottish, you know. We're fundraising for an archaeological excavation to unearth the Holy Grail, close to Rosslyn Chapel, or if it's not there, somewhere in Lanark. Alasdair Gray might know where. Would you like to make a donation?
  Ah sort o' ken where Lanark is, an' dinnae ken whae the Gray chap is; never heard o' him. Ah've heard o' Muriel Gray. No thanks, son.

* Knock, knock.
  Who's there?
  Ma.
  Ma who?
  Ma Scoatish workin class credenshuls ur better than yoors.

* Knock, knock.
  Who's there?
  Al.
  Al who?
  Al outdo yi wi ma Scoatish workin class credenshuls.

* Why did the Scottish Jacobite Party Member cross the road? To avoid the Scottish Communist Party Member who was storming towards him to enlighten him about certain impracticalities and the proletariat.

* How many Red Clydesiders would it have taken to change a light bulb? Only John Maclean could've given you the Leninist line on that one.

* How many Red Clydesiders would it have taken to change a light bulb? There would be no need. The light from Lenin's skull would prove enough.

* 'Dear Marcuse, how are things in Hades? Here's a probing one for you. How many arguing couples nowadays does it take to change a ceiling GU10 LED light bulb?'
  'Dear Orwell, commitment is often a challenge for the postmodern marriage, but – as I've said – not every problem is necessarily due to the Capitalist mode of production.'

* What's truly special about a traditional Marxist Christmas dinner? After the giant Waitrose turkey with all the trimmings, the trifle, and the brandy, comes the two-hour Marxist diatribe about the power of consumer Capitalism and turkey fetishism.

Intellectuals: So superior

* How many left intellectuals does it take to change a light bulb? Ah, they'd sooner change us, the great unillumined, the eternally duped according to their lights. They never switch off or flicker, cannot unscrew in their dismal, hermeneutic cells. The intellectual elect, we can never change them.

* Michel Foucault walks into a pub with a rare exotic parrot on his shoulder and, behind him, the Ayatollah Khomeini.

  Al Murray, the pub landlord, says in an aside: 'What are we to make of this?'

  The parrot squawks: 'Bliss was it in that Dawn to be alive.'

* Two Greek anarchists are making Molotov cocktails. One says to the other, 'So who will we throw these at then?'
The other replies, 'What are you, some kind of f****** intellectual?!?'

* How many neo-Marxist historians does it take to change an Eveready Rough Service light bulb?
'Change it? No, not the same old. It must be revealed for what it was and is – patriotic, submissive, and rough – then confidently chided and shamed, and told to be that which it failed to be – an all-illuminating Gramscian light bulb, like this one here in my hand, in the imprisoning darkness.'

* Er, excuse me, I'd like to speak up in defence of the benighted old Eveready bulb! Here goes. How many historicist historians (Old School ... non-judgemental) does it take to change a light bulb? Five (there's not many more than that): one to say how good the old one was, one to replace it with another old one, one to say how it continues to make us wiser about humankind, one to state that it allows us to see the present more clearly, and one to stand guard against a Gramscian or Foucaultian bulb being used, as those are far too bright. Touché?

* The Broons are at home, in Dundee; they're on the inter-web, and looking at Bella Caledonia's Scots dialect pages (jings!):
  'Help ma' boab. Hey, Horace, whit's "tak tent" mean, … an' "wunner", … an' "schule", an' "dominie", an' "Oor European Leid"; an' a "scriever", whit's that?'
  'Crivens, ah've nae idea, Joe. It's aw Greek tae us, or wiz it Doric? Daphne, did yi no' hae' a pal at school called Bella Cameron?'

* **How do you spot a left-liberal intellectual?**

Shock-headed Marxists chewing polysyllables
(George Orwell, *The Road to Wigan Pier, 1937; Penguin, 1975)*

It's easy. They have more front than Selfridges.

It's called 'insouciance'. Insouciance? Think of nonchalance.

They deploy terms and concepts from left field. They inveigle the words 'subversion' and 'empowerment' into the conversation, and 'critique', and 'storied'. You're not familiar with these terms. You are disempowered by this ploy.

They frolic in a kind of word field.

They 'decode' art. It's unnerving.

They use the word 'transgress'.

They soon slip in the term 'Binary Opposition'.

Nick Cohen calls them bovine.

Yon Seamus has a lean and hungry look.

They use the word 'liminal'. It's not an easy word to find out about.

You'll hear the term 'patriarchy'. Beware of this, and Bea Campbell.

They slip in the word 'agency'. It throws you.

They might use the word 'transmogrify'. This throws you. It's a standard ploy – you have to think what the word means, so that shuts you up. You are disempowered by this trick. I'm still wondering what the 'mogri' part of this verb means.

They use the word 'space' a great deal. Think of the word 'heterotopia'. That's what it means.

They use the word 'deconstruct' a lot. I've heard one say: 'Anandi designed a deconstructed pinstripe suit for women.'

Melanie Phillips is a good guide. She clocks them right away, and says, 'Can we dispense with the jargon?'

Gosh, the words soon get under your skin. I used the terms 'valorise' and 'discourse' the other day! I was trying to explain. My, it's certainly hip knowing these things.

Presenting critiquing Art or History programmes on TV, they're resorting to an autocue. They are cheating. If he or she is photogenic, that compels even more.

The young ones are but excitable children with Foucaultian sweets. Too much of Foucault's sugar has rendered them hyper-active.

There's that wince word: 'intertextuality'.

Sonia is studying Masculinity in Ancient Sparta at LSE. ... No, sorry, I got that wrong. She's studying the LSE itself now. Her thesis is entitled: 'Institutionalised Masculinity at LSE'.

Mark is studying Selfian Psychogeography and Flaneurism at LSE.

Tariq is doing a PhD on the Origins of Radical Strolling at LSE.

Leo's thesis at the School of Oriental & African Studies is entitled: 'The Benin Empire as Empire Par Excellence'.

Akram's PhD at the School of Oriental & African Studies is entitled: 'Akbar the Great and the Chittor Massacre: A Belated Revision.'

At Leicester University's Museum Studies Department, Aadita's PhD is entitled 'Composing the Dramaturgy: Achieving the Liminal Experience from the Outside, Betwixt-and-Between the Normal'.

At Manchester Museum's Art Gallery & Museum Studies, Beverley's PhD is entitled: 'The Liminality and Rhetoric of the Anti-Thatcherite Slogan "What Do We Want & When Do We Want It?!"'

They speak in texts, grand texts – not like our piddling texts, such as 'i82 chocolate eclairs 2 day at t break' or 'omg he's fit! KPC', or 'my favourite Dylan track is "To Ramona"'; more like: 'All human history is Text, as is the world, and knowledge itself. Let us read the text.' I have to think OMG! when I hear that.

'Oh, la-de-da-de-da', as my mother would have said.

✳ The Artist-Legislator as future Minister, 2020

Will Self: UK Minister for Intelligent Strolling

A. L. Kennedy: Government Liaison Secretary for the Inaugural Artist as Legislator Forum

Emma Thompson: Minister for Cultural Transitioning – Isle of Wight

The Reverend Richard Coles: Secretary for Broadcasting Right-On Right Thinking

Simon Armitage: Green Minister for Coastal Walks & Vital Rumination

Lemn Sissay: Chancellor of the Gossamer Light Moral Imperative

Akala: Minister Without Portfolio for the Elucidation of Chomsky Through Rap

Carol Ann Duffy: Secretary for the Dissemination of *The Alternative British* History Through Rap, Period I: 1066 to 2020 general election

Grayson Perry: Commissar for the Establishment of The People's Revolutionary Calendar & Public Holidays – To Be Introduced May Day, 2021

Kate Tempest: Minister for Transcendent Rap

Mark Steel: Commissar for Inveiglement of Young Audiences on BBC Radio 4

David Olusoga: Secretary-Divine for the Disabusing of Cherished British Notions

Lord Melvyn Bragg of Northbore Chipdom-Muddlebrow: Diviner of THE NORTH (Don)

Grayson Perry: Commissioner for the Reconstruction of the White English Middle-Class Male, 2025–2030

✳ **Poet Members of Parliament at their constituency surgery**

Alicia Fletcher, MSP, Scottish Socialist Party, Muirhouse surgery, Edinburgh West:
'Ali, thurs u wee fuckin hoody ayeways sprayin ANURCHY! an FOOCKO NOW an VOTE YES OR ELSE oan the sido oor flats. Ah umnae goanti thi polis ugain. Uh want action.'
'Betty, hen, uhm wi yi oan this. I shall get my son, Noam, to ensure that he gets the phonetics right in future; or if it's my daughter, Rosa, ditto.'

Ben Okri, sage poet as Legislator, and Scotophile, has come to Caledonia; MSP, Scottish National Party, 2021, Muirhouse surgery, Edinburgh West:
'Ben, thurs u big fuckin hoody sprayin ANARKI 4 UZ an' CHOMPSKY NOW oan thi sido oor flats. Yur predecessur didnae stoap it.'
'Betty, what I offer will work like a charm. Here is what you do: Allow uncontemplated regions/ Of time to project themselves/Into your sleeping consciousness,/ Inducing terror, or mental liberation. "Mental fight" is what we need. Here, take this: my book.'
'Ur yi huvin mi oan? Nun o this hairy fairy stuff iz gonnae work.'

Saul Farley, Left Unity councillor, Princes Park ward surgery, Liverpool:

Saul, there's been the most awful black and red ANARCHY! graffiti sprayed on the gable ends of our street, Inkerman Terrace. What can you do about it?'

'Well, Mrs Callaghan, it sounds rather crude. The answer, as always in an alienating, neo-liberal world, is the right aesthetic. Theresa and Godwin from the Art and Literature departments of John Moores University will be in touch about coming along to Inkerman Terrace to develop the graffiti further, in line with the city's Public Art, Outreach & Well-Being Guidelines. A large figure of Rosa Luxembourg might be added and Godwin may include a line from Shelley or Bakunin. We think you'll like the finished result.'

'Radio Luxembourg? Godwin who? Mr Farley, I'm hard of hearing, and I don't know who these figures are.'

Soviet Russia and other dead ends

* How many Stalinists does it take to change a light bulb? One to petition the Ministry of Light for a bulb, fifty to establish the state production quota, two hundred militia to force the factory unions to allow production of the bulb, and one to surreptitiously dial an '800' number to order an American light bulb.

* How many Poles does it take to change a light bulb? Just one, but you need six thousand Russian troops in case he goes on strike!

* How can you use a banana as a compass? Place a banana on the Berlin Wall. East is where a bite has been taken out of it.

* Knock, knock.
  Who's there?
  Stasi!

* Rabbi, can one build Socialism in one country?
  Yes, my son, but one must live in another.
  (Anon, The Spectator, 1984)

* Two Russian nudists are sitting on a porch. It's 1989.
  Perestroika is well underway.
  One says to the other, 'I say, old boy, have you read
  Marx?'
  His friend replies, 'Yes, I believe it's these wicker
  chairs.'

* What is Socialism? It is the longest and rockiest road
  from Capitalism back to Capitalism.

* How many Cubans does it take to change a Capitalist
  energy efficient light bulb?
  'Bugger the light bulbs. We need an energy plan, and
  not a Russian one.'

* How many Venezuelans does it take to change a Capitalist energy efficient light bulb?
  'First they need to be distributed. At least we've got an energy plan now, and it's not a Russian plan, or a Cuban one.'

* Castro says he probably won't be around in four years. The news caused a 35 percent drop in the stock price of Havana Rafts and Inner Tubes.

* How many Red Guards does it take to change a light bulb?
  '. . . Quick, hide the light bulb.'

* How many Chairman of the Chinese Communist Party does it take to change a light bulb? . . . Shall we pass them one of the three thousand square-shaped Tiananmen commemorative light bulbs? Mmm, better not flick that one on.

* How many Chairman of the Chinese Communist Party does it take to change a light bulb? China?! Communist Party-managed-State Capitalism? Explaining the glories and spec of the Energy Star LED 3M-PAR 38-Y3 light bulb would be easier, I can tell you.

* What's a definition of the unlikely? British communists opting to live in Cuba, China, North Korea, Russia, or Greece.

* How many Brahmins does it take to change a light bulb? An Infinite number. One to change the bulb, twenty to form the light bulb workers' union (Secularist-Marxist), thirty to form the counter union (Hindutvadin), one to be the light bulb minister, one to head the Light Bulb Corporation, thirty to be nominated to the Light Bulb Corporation, one hundred to go to USA and Europe to import product surveys on purchasing light bulbs, three to form the judicial Enquiry commission on light bulb scandals ... and so on.

The new norm:
It's not bright

* How many politically correct liberals does it take to change a light bulb? 3,500. One to do it and 3,499 to make sure that they do it in such a way that can be observed as non-racist, sexist, or elitist.

* How many liberals does it take to change a light bulb? None. They believe that if they call the light bulb a racist long enough, they'll force the light bulb to change itself. (Lawrence Person)

* The attendees of an LSE Critical Theory Colloquium and a Plain English Society AGM just happened to end up in the same pub. They got chatting, critically and plainly. Al Murray, the pub landlord, sensed trouble (PES is pro-Orwell, as is Al Murray now). To prevent a right verbal punch-up ensuing, he provided what the former called for: 'a cordon sanitaire of chairs'. This brought the reply

from one of the PES: 'They're bar stools, call them bar stools, plain and simple.'

* How many post-processual archaeologists does it take to change a light bulb? All of them: one to change the bulb, and the rest to ensure that their dissertations on the observed phenomenon all comply with the strictures of neo-Marxist theory.

* I would not want to offend or belittle one single ant, an ant colony, or indeed the ant community, but that Steve Backshall, the Wildlife presenter chap, is he an anti-civ anarchist by any chance? I've been wondering what the ant community would make of an insurrecto ant in their midst.

* **That Chris Packham, the naturalist . . .**

He's got a book coming out. It's his counter-blast to Plato's *Republic*. It's entitled *Primate's Republic*, published by Verso Press; to be followed by *Playtpus Republic*, *Pelican's Republic*, ad infinitum . . . and finally: *Plankton's Republic*. He is Philosopher King for the animal world.

Chris Packham is patron of a sage owl, you know. He calls it 'Socrates, my Socrates'.

What's the difference between a social primate and Chris Packham? The chimpanzee isn't anti-globalisation and misanthropic.

What's the difference between an owl and Chris Packham? The wise owl would vote for a mainstream MP, even if Chris Packham was voting for a Machiavellian barn owl, and the wise owl knows there are plenty of those. Two claws and one beak good? Two legs, a small nose, and Parliamentary Acts bad? The wise owl needs no thesis on that one.

The BBC's naturalists department have formed a political party. Their first MPs in the 2020 general election might well be the easy-going, pacifist orangutang, and the sage barn owl.

The cerebral ones: Try the theory. It's still dark

* Did you hear the one about the Llandudno Marxist who opened a small electrical shop? He named it Dai Electrical Materials.

* Doctor, Doctor, I've got Marxist compulsive dialectical materialism disorder. What can I do?
  Well, my thesis is – up the ante.

* Doctor, Doctor, I've got compulsive dialectical materialism disorder. What can I do?
  Well, my thesis is – meet yourself halfway, that'll resolve it.

* Doctor, Doctor, I've got compulsive dialectical materialism disorder. What can you give me for it?
  Take this dystopia. Up the dosage if it gets worse.

* Doctor, doctor, I've absorbed so many lefty mantras in my head I don't think I can cope now.
Mmm, sounds quite a cloistered condition. Try first a dose of self-subjugation, if that doesn't work move onto self-flagellation, and if no difference, then check into a monastery. If no joy there, then resort to a White Privileging retreat. They're big on purgatives.

* How many Critical Theorists does it take to change a light bulb? Only one, but first he has to sit in a darkened room and determine whether light is something he really needs or if it's just something that's been culturally imposed upon him.

* How many Critical Theorists does it take to change a light bulb?
'I find it symptomatic of a lacuna in your thinking that you choose to privilege the crude quantitative analysis over the logically prior ontological enquiry.'

* A PhD in English Literature & Society walks into his local pub, The Olde Bank of England, near the LSE. The intellectually keen Al Murray, the pub landlord, says to him:
'Hello, Patrick. A pint of the best James Joyce?'
'Certainly, Al.'

... 'Now, Patrick, I've been thinking about what you were saying last week, about the particular "space" you are examining, the pub, and I would argue that the public house belongs to that set of unique spaces Michel Foucault terms "heterotopia". They are spaces that buck the architectural, political, or spatial norms of the time and in so doing articulate cultural engagement with being.'

'Wow, Al, what an epiphany! Gosh!'

* How many radical solipsists does it take to change a light bulb? Just one. No one else exists. (I get this, but I can't know if all the other solipsists do.)

* How many postmodernists does it take to change a light bulb? Two. One to ponder the subtextualities of change regarding the cultural hegemony of the electrical/manual pseudo duality, and one to call the janitor.

* 'Excuse me, Dr Wahner: How many Deconstructionists does it take to change a light bulb?' 'Ah, you must read my book: *Benedikt Wahner, Reflections on "Deconstruction" and (Formal) Logics.*'

* Oh, honestly. 'Plus ingenii quam sapientiae': 'More brains than sense', as my mother would have said.

* 'Dear Marcuse, how are things in Hell today? Here's a probing one. How many self-harmers does it take to change a light bulb?'
  'Dear Hitchens, have you been talking to George Orwell by any chance? ... It's a similar answer: yes, not every problem is due to the neo-liberal economy and globalisation.'

* 'Dear Marcuse, how are things in Hell today? Here's another one for you. How many young Cultural Marxists does it take to change a ceiling GU10 LED light bulb?'
  'Dear Hitchens, I shall outsmart you on this occasion. Give me a minute. ...... Two. One to *eventually* get it in, and one to say: There you are. Herbert Marcuse was right. We are slaves to Capitalism's bulb designers.'

* 'Dear Marcuse, Hitchens here. Here is my retort to yours of last week, which ended '... slaves to Capitalism's bulb designers'. Jane, who eventually got the tricky ceiling LED light bulb in, using the green rubber Capitalist sucker thing (what a blessing!), says: 'Brad, like fuck off, man. Man up.'

* How many Islington neo-Zapatistas does it take to transfigure a Capitalist light bulb? Two: one to fit on a transcendent Marcos-balaclava-design lampshade from Homefresh, Covent Garden, and one to recite, in Ancient Mayan, their anti-commodification cryptic chant on behalf of the Subcomandante's woollen mask: 'We Are You, We Are You.'

Uni/higher education: Foucault rules

* How many Foucault lecturers does it take to change a light bulb? None, they just hold the bulb in the air and world revolves around them.

* What do you call an institution where parrots learn Critical Theory? Polytechnique Foucault.

* How can you tell if a parrot is intelligent? It speaks in poly-Foucault syllables.

* How can you tell if a parrot is intelligent? It speaks Foucaultese fluently.

* How can you tell if a parrot is intelligent? It speaks Critical Theory rote fashion.

* Teach a parrot to say 'Foucault's concept of "empowering exhibitionism"' and you have a Critical Theory student.

* Foucault's concept of 'the Archive' is more easily described by what it is not than by what it is.

* While you might readily get a public art gallery curator and museum keeper to say 'Foucault's concept of "empowering exhibitionism"' (especially in London), you won't get an archivist to say 'Foucault's concept of "the Archive"', I can tell you, especially in Manchester and Salford.

Twelve wisecracks from the Anglosphere

USA:

* How many lefty moonbats does it take to change a light bulb? None. They'd rather sit in the dark and blame George W. Bush.

* What do the initials UCSC stand for? University of Counter-cultural Spoiled Children.

* What do you call ten thousand US liberals fleeing to Canada? A good start.

Canada:

* What do you call ten thousand US liberals arriving in Canada? An argument for cheap return fares for ten thousand US liberals? Or an opportunity for a fair exchange? We'll take five thousand – no Jane Fonda – and give you one hundred Toronto liberals, and add fifty Halifax anarchists? And, please, can we throw in Donald Sutherland? And Naomi Klein?

Australia:

* Did you hear the old joke about Australian Communist Party membership and the membership levels for Aussie political parties generally? Ex-communists were Australia's largest political party.

* How many executives of the Builders Labourers Federation does it take to change a light bulb? '... You wouldn't have put that provocative question to comrade Norm Gallagher, I can tell you.'

* What do you get if you cross a Melbourne situationist with a Mafioso? A guy who makes you an offer you can't understand, but Mayor Doyle sure likes the street artwork.

* What do you get if you cross a sexagenarian Sydney Push situationist with a Mafioso? A guy who makes you an offer you can't understand, and who says, nostalgically, he knew Germaine Greer when she was a member, and Clive James.

New Zealand:

* What do you get if you cross an Auckland situationist with a Mafioso? A guy who makes you a street mural you can't refuse, and never asked for, don't like, and can't get rid of.

* What do you get if you cross a sexagenarian Christchurch situationist with a Mafioso? A guy who makes you an offer you can't understand, and who says, nostalgically, he knew the great Bill 'Ubi' Dwyer in the 1960s ... and who adds he shouldn't be saying that as true Situationists are anti-nostalgia.

Ireland:

* How many Provisional Sinn Fein members does it take to change a light bulb? You'll have to ask their think tank on light bulbs first.

An anarcha-feminist, a Catholic feminist, and a Tory feminist . . .

* An anarcha-feminist, a Catholic feminist, a Tory feminist, a SlutWalk feminist, Beyoncé, and Mary Berry walk into a pub together.
  The astute pub landlord, the clued-up Al Murray, says: 'What is this, some kind of joke?'

* Jane Garvey, scold us, chide me. Teach us to be free.

* How many radical feminists does it take to change a light bulb?
  '. . . That's not funny, abusive white male aggressor.'

* How many radical feminists does it take to screw in a light bulb? Eight:-

> one to suggest the whole 'screwing' bit is too 'rape-like'

> one to add that it endorses patriarchal 'rape culture'

> one to deconstruct the light bulb itself as being phallic

> one to blame men for not changing the bulb

> one to blame men for trying to change the bulb instead of letting a woman do it

> one to blame men for creating a society that discourages women from changing light bulbs

> one to blame men for creating a society where women change too many light bulbs

> and one to advocate that light bulb changers should have wage parity with electricians.

* How many male feminists does it take to change a light bulb? Just one, but he has to watch his wife do the cooking and cleaning first.

* How many male feminists does it take to change a light bulb? None, because they already see the light, while they stumble in the dark.

* Why shouldn't you let a man's mind wander? Because it's way too little to be out all alone. (thoughtcatalog.com/30 hilarious jokes for feminists)

* What's the fastest way to a man's heart? Through his chest with a sharp knife. (thoughtcatalog.com/30 hilarious jokes for feminists)

* What do you get if you cross the maverick US feminist Camille Paglia with the Scottish Conservative leader, MSP, and feminist Ruth Davidson? A rare breed: a special steer, a lonely steer that's worth the following.

How do you spot a left-liberal intellectual?

They frolic in a kind of phrase-garden

How can you tell if a parrot is intelligent?

It speaks in poly-Foucault syllables

How many Corbyn cabinet ministers does it take to change a 10 Downing Street light bulb ? (The janitor has quit, and so has the cat).

There's no point. The Nationalised grid has been down for weeks.

Collective nouns for leftists:

A sanctum of socialists.

Collective nouns for leftists

A cuckoo's nest of Cultural Marxists

Tricky Mrs Pankhurst

Mr. Left perplexed : Mr. Right correct ?

I don't believe it - she couldn't, could she? - surely it's only the left that empowers women? She's not as great as Germaine Greer. so she was a social conservative then.

- she hated Bolsheviks and attacks on property
- she hated Lenin
- one of her daughters 'lived in sin' with an Italian anarchist
- she was critical of mass trade union power, following the 1926 General Strike.

Mrs Pankhurst:
Goodness me.
She turned Tory.
Let her be.
You can't fault her pedigree.
'Tricky' Mrs Pankhurst.

Annus Corbynilis: 2015

* Ed Miliband is sitting disconsolately in a pub one night in early September.
  Come chucking-out time Al Murray, the pub landlord, says to him: 'Come on, Ed, it's later than you think. Lights out.'

* Jeremy Corbyn walks into the same pub the following day; a few steps behind him is Derek Hatton.
  The highly principled Al Murray, the pub landlord, shouts out: 'Hatton, you're still barred.'

* Which of these new posts might Derek Hatton be given in the Corbyn government of 2020–2025 (oops, 2017–)?

> UK Buffet Organiser for Syriza Visit.
> Ambassador: Gents Loo Diplomacy.
> Adviser to Militant Tendency Wide Boys.
> Minister for Bike-less Enterprise
> Minister for Unfree Enterprise
> Minister for Charm
> Minister for Liverpool Taxis
> Minister for Municipal Taxis
> Minister for National Income Taxes: England, Wales & Northern Ireland.
> Overseas Minister Without Portfolio: Hijacking Reformist Bourgeoisie Parties
> National Secretary for Candle Banks.

* How many Corbyn cabinet ministers does it take to change a 10 Downing Street light bulb? (The janitor has quit, and so has the cat.) There's no point. The Nationalised grid has been down for weeks.

A number of ways to make Jeremy Corbyn more exciting:

Have him:

> say to Jeremy Paxman: 'Jeremy, that's simply rude.'
>
> buy his Coco silk-satin pyjama set from Selfridges.
>
> buy lots of nice new office stationery.
>
> hang out with Gilbert & George.
>
> support Coventry City FC or, better still, New Mills FC, or Arsenal.

Top Corbynite political turn-ons:

Lenin arriving at Finlyandsky Station Terminus, St. Petersburg, in 1917.

Organic mushy peas ... or rather – non-organic mushy peas.

The two dog breeds: the proletarian pointer, and the Tory terrier.

Scottish communist miners, any decade: in The North North.

Welsh communist miners, any decade: in The West North.

Cardiff communist miners, any decade: in The South Wales North.

Kent miners, 1984–1985 Miners' Strike: in The South Coast/English Channel North.

Marx Terrace, Chopwell, Tyne and Wear: in The North or the North-East North.

Seamus Milne's *Guardian* connections.

Maxine Peak as Watt Tyler at Manchester's Royal Exchange theatre: in The North?

You might be a Corbynite if . . .

You think the proletariat is both imminent and immanent, and especially strong in a particular country . . . like Cuba, and The North.

You have named your kids Rosa, Watt, Che, Noam, or Maxine.

You make no distinction between 'ought to be' and 'is'.

You have ever thought Jesus was en route to being a Socialist but succumbed to 'false consciousness' and turned to the Resurrection, creating, thereby, the opium of the masses ... that Jesus, son of a carpenter, was therefore a class traitor of truly historic proportions, and extremely narcissistic and self-absorbed ... call it a Messiah complex.

When people say 'Marx' you think 'Moses', or 'Messiah'. But the Communist Manifesto is not the Ten Commandments.

You don't like Voltaire on free-speech.

You came of age in the 1960s and heckled Bob Dylan in Manchester when he 'sold out'.

After the giant Tesco Christmas turkey with all the trimmings, the trifle, and the brandy, comes your lengthy Marxist diatribe about the power of consumer Capitalism and turkey fetishism.

You hate gentrification in Islington and Hackney but treat yourself and fellow Corbynites to lunch in the new bijou restaurant. There's plenty of these in The North actually.

Annus Corbynilis/ horribilis: 2016

How many Corbynites does it take to change light bulb?
'. . . All the membership, and we're giving the bulb to Jeremy now.'

How many members of Momentum does it take to change a light bulb?
'. . . We know where you live.'

How many members of Momentum does it take to change a light bulb?
'. . . Might one thrust suffice to switch your lights off?'

How many Corbynites does it take to screw in a light bulb? Well, it took one Ed Miliband to screw up the Labour Party.

The moniker for … ?
(Spot the Trot)

* In his heady Cambridge years – the moniker for
  Andrew Marr: 'Red Andy'.
  Well, there's many a sparkling career began with
  shandy.

* In his youthful student days – the moniker for
  Chancellor Darling: 'Trot Alistersky LLB'?
  Well – studentsky unions: just young Trots on the
  spree.

* In her post-Trotskyphilia days – the moniker for
  Paymaster Primarolo: 'Red Dawn', then 'Red Dawn
  Rising'.
  Oh, dear. Well, it's just the press. It's not surprising.

* In his latter trotting days – a moniker for Christopher
  Hitchens: 'Pink Popinjay'? 'Pink Hitch'?
  Well, farewell dazzling apostate, former Marxist titch.

* In his bold Workers' Power Group years – the moniker
  for Marxist journalist, Paul Mason:
  '. . . Look, I might've had one. That was a long time
  ago. Let this statement suffice now, okay: I Am Not A
  Revolutionary Marxist!'

* In his tilting student days – the moniker for Philip
  Dunn?: 'No Trident Phil'? 'Mutual Assured
  Destruction Phil'? 'High Horse Phil'?
  Well, there's many a high horse. And Rocinante had
  his fill.

Collective nouns and adjectives for leftists

A sanctum of socialists

A narcissisium of socialists

A huddle of socialists

A scowl of socialists

A department of Marxists

A symposium of louche, languid Greek Marxists

A cuckoo's nest of Cultural Marxists

A rumpus room of Occupiers

A meme of anti-Globalisers

One lone, unpopular relativist

One lonely nihilist. He shuns the collective

One wandering radical solipsist. He occasionally tries the collective

The last Class War activist. Stuff the collective

A relic of socialists

A schism of socialists

A shibboleth of socialists

A mantra of Marxists

A murmuration of Trotskyites

A synthesis of Liberation Theologists

A scuttle of social justice warriors

Among the world's shortest books

The Soviet Guide to Tunnelling

The Chinese Communist Party's Manual on Dealing with Student Protests

Emigrating to Cuba

A Socialist Guide to Living in Cuba

Ballet Careers in Cuba

Career Opportunities in Greece

The North Korean Telephone Directory

The Socialist Guide to Democratic Participation

The Socialist Guide to Tolerance

The Marxist Guide to Freedom of Speech

The Soviet Union Guide to Critical Theory

Left Apologists for Communist Tyranny, by Noam Chomsky

A Guide to Ensuring Solidarity Across Syriza; with a one-sentence Foreword by Jeremy Corbyn and a two-sentence Introduction by Ken Loach and Paul Mason.

A Socialist Guide to Dress Code for Labour Party General Election TV Broadcasts, by Jo Brand.

Alternative & unofficial national anthems

(some offer several choices)

The Soviet Union: Old Joe Stalin Had a Farm; I Aint Gonna Work on Stalin's Farm No More; Big Bad Jo

The German Democratic Republic: Ten Green Bottles Hanging on the Wall; We Gotta Get Out Of This Place; Born to Run; 18 With a Bullet

Soviet Bloc Hungary: The Party's Over; Bad Moon Rising

Soviet Bloc Czechoslovakia: Send in the Tanks

Soviet Bloc Romania: Breaking Up is Hard to Do

Soviet Bloc Poland, 1980–1983: The Mighty Lech; Food, Glorious Food. Either of these could alternate with the Polish National anthem of 1797, the pro-Napoleon 'Poland Is Not Yet Lost' (Mazurek Dąbrowskiego)

Cuba: Born Free; Row, Row, Row Your Boat; Somewhere Over the Rainbow; Dancing in the Dark

China: Walk a Mile in My Shoes; Send In The Tanks; China In Your Hands (by T'Pau); Chains (Carole King); I Feel Free (Cream); Try a Little Tenderness; I Say a Little Prayer; Slow Down; Hard to Handle (Patti Drew)

North Korea: You Are My Sunshine, My Only Sunshine; Express Yourself; Suspicious Minds

Democratic Kampuchea: Born Under a Bad Sign

Laos People's Democratic Republic: Stuck in the Middle

Greece: Rescue Me

Scotland: Nicola, Ya Belter (lyrics by The Proclaimers; tune, Gloria, by permission of Van Morrison)

Songs for the followers

California in the 1960s: Voices Green and Purple, by The Bees, 1966; N.S.U., by Cream, 1966.

Toronto's Green and SlutWalk protests, 2011–2016: Voices Green and Purple.

Pennsylvania, 2016 US Election: Swing to the Right, by Utopia, 2013.

'Herland', a prospective hidden feminist ecovillage somewhere in Latin America: Purple Haze, by Jimi Hendrix, 1967.

United Kingdom, 2008–2020: Tubthumping, by Chumbawamba; Fuck Off – Rip Off, by Chumbawamba; … okay then, virtually anything by Chumbawamba, 1986–2012; St Anger, by Metallica; the BBC commissioned musical 'The Levellers', by Andrew Lloyd Webber & Brian May (history consultant to Les Levs, Billy Bragg), 2019, being an adaption of the *Guardian*-commissioned poem by Toni Harrison (in 649 heroic couplets), 'The Levellers and the Gorgon', 2017.

On May Day 2020 Chumbawamba re-grouped to protest against the Webber & May 'Les Levs' production as being too 'saccharine', and insisted that the title of the Harrison poem become the name of the musical. Billy Bragg was non-committal.

Counter graffiti, slogans, and insults

Better Red than Dead – Better Fed Than Reds And Better Read

When There Is No Vision The People Perish – When There Are Ivory Towers the Idealists Live In Cloud-Cuckoo-Land

The Tigers Of Wrath Are Wiser Than The Horses Of Instruction – My, This Grass Hopper of Wisdom Is Just An Anarchist Pussycat. The Confucian Horses Are Gainfully Employed At Least. Tigers Just Burn Bright.

I Fought The Law – And The Clash Made A Fortune Out Of The Phrase

Eat The Rich – Boil An Anarchist For Two Days. Add A Generous Dose Of Pepper

Cats Like Plain Crisps – The Tigers Of Wrath Like Kendal Mint Cake

No Gods, No Country, No Masters! – No Trains, No Buses, No Trafalgar Square Then For Your Small Demonstration.

Another World Is Possible – Try Another Planet, Mate

SPREAD ANARCHY – DON'T TELL ME WHAT TO DO!

PLANET NOT PROFIT – PROFIT NEEDS PLANTING

Six Years Of Forced, Fear-Driven Austerity Has United The People! – Yes, all 0.16 % Of The People

We Are Many – Actually, Well Below 1% of The UK Population

To Change Everything, Start Anywhere – To Change Something, Start Somewhere First

Religion Is The Opium Of The Masses – Revolution Is The Opium Of The Intellectuals

'The British Road to Socialism' – The British Road To Lost Deposits More Like?

Here's Tae Us. Wha's Like Us? – Maist Folk.

'The Museum Of Communism' – Above McDonald's, Na Prikope 10, Prague

It's The Oil, Stupid – It's A Lefty Myth, Stupid.

O Say Can You See my Democracy? – O Say Can You See My Hypocrisy?

The worst advertisement for Socialism is its adherents.
(George Orwell, *The Road to Wigan Pier*, 1937; Penguin, 1975)

You call that statesmanship? I call it an emotional spasm.
(Aneurin Bevan on demands within the Labour Party for unilateral nuclear disarmament, 1957)

Every communist has a fascist frown; every fascist has a communist smile (Muriel Spark, *The Girls of Slender Means*, 1963; Penguin, 1966)

Anti-Capitalists? Just a bunch of edgy teenagers.

Excitable children with Foucaultian sweets. Too much of Foucault's sugar has rendered you hyper-active.

Plus ingenii quam sapientiae: More brains than sense.

How can you tell if a parrot is intelligent? It speaks Critical Theory rote fashion.

You are all merely turned into tongues.

You are a parrot teacher.

Thicko, Brexit thickos?
Guess what? I'm with thicko.
Guess what? I'm big at Kew.
Get this: I'm with thicko.
Guess why? He's not like you.

V For Vendetta – Does Your Mum Know You Wear The Sinister Guy Fawkes Mask?

V For Vendetta – It Puts People Off!

V For Vendetta – V For Vacuous

V For Vendetta – V For Vamoose

V For Vendetta – V For Vandalism

V For Vendetta – V For Vile

V For Vendetta – V For Vindictive Left

V For Vendetta – V For Vaccination: discovered by the English doctor, Edward Jenner

V For Vendetta – V For Victory

V For Vendetta – V For Vote in the Brexit referendum

V For Vendetta ~ Vengeance is sweet

Aphorisms

Blessed are they that run round in circles, for they shall be known as Corbynites taken by surprise.

Least said, the sooner the PC apparatchiks mend us.

A lefty cannot change his spots.

More socialist than thou.

Whoso discovereth George Orwell findeth a good thing.

There is nothing new under the Socialist sun.

The more things change the less they look like a Socialist Republic.

Bliss was it in that dawn to be alive, but to be young ... er, that had something to do with it.

A spectacle is amusing Tories no end – the spectacle of Corbynism.

The Marxists have always sought to change the world, in conflicting ways; the point is to interpret it correctly.

Water is much too serious a thing to be left to Marxist mandarins.

Every communist has a fascist frown (Muriel Spark, *The Girls of Slender Means*, 1963; Penguin, 1966)

To think is to be a Marxist apparently, to control divine.

A little Marxism is a mischievous thing.

A little Marxist is a creepy thing.

From each according to his financial plan, to each according to his wants.

Take care of the pennies and the luxuries will follow.

My examined life is certainly worth living, thanks to prosperity.

Most learned of barbers *(Doctissime Tonsorum)*, please counsel Jeremy Corbyn.

Where there was no Council, Militant held sway.

A Miliband answer is a little dark cloudlet.

A Corbyn answer doth not entertain the question.

Whoso cometh upon Burke's *Reflections* in later life findeth a most pertinent thing.

Let correction standeth: the reflective angels and saints have many a rich polemic and quote. Do Paine and Shelley partake of the devil's polemic?

Reason is a rational way of going wrong with confidence.

And why are you happy to hear leftist scorn? Consider the stand-ups of the left, how they pose; they love nought, neither do they mature. And I say to you, that even Bill Gates with all his causes is not acclaimed by one of them. (Matthew 6:28–29)

Verse

i

It's Tom Paine this, Tom Paine that.

What did he do later?

Drew up plans for Bonaparte.

What a little traitor.

ii

Socialism?

God give me Stoicism.

iii

CT:

This foreign hatching needs some genius nonce.

Well, there's 'Cuckoo Theory'; that's my response.

iv

When PC rules, we won't be glad.

We'll have to check our mum and dad.

v

The lefties cannot change their spots.
Few hide them better than the Trots.

vi

It ends up scatological.
It's less the dialectical
And more the pathological.

vii

A. L. Kennedy =
Diva of the Pompous.
Marxist rhombus as Moral Compass.
Paragon? Sage? Or niggle?
I want to giggle.

viii

So, Farewell then
Ed Miliband.
The £3 membership fee
Was a brain wave.
Will we ever see you again,
Do you think?

ix

Well, Hello then
Jeremy Corbyn.
How did this happen?
Jeremiad
Would have liked you.
Behold, Jezza,
Your People's Austerity
Laid out before you
Like a Promised Land.

x

Some archaeologists, what are they like!
Think student-Rousseauesque, think Woodstock- vibe;
Cogito cuckoo-like, and sweet nestlings;
Think spoon-fed Ologies, their ziggurat –
Phenomenology; think pieties,
And the sainthood of one's reflexive self.
Think polarised – though as instructive aim.
Their impresarios make mighty claims:
Here's a Pompeii, and there's a Mary Rose.
I'd say they're lording it: aggrandisement
Is here at play, yet Ozymandias,
Their shibboleth, must never cross their minds.
Long-spoofed, the New Tuition's ages old:
Γινώσκω Aristophanes' Thinkery.
Perhaps he'd add – 'And now? Think Dialectic Weaponised'.

xi

The news is too much with us; let us prune
The Daily Glut and regain our powers.
Yes, doom's abroad, and who has gloom like ours.
This couch potato says: don't blame the spoon.
This island State part blest by Empire's boon,
Our Parliament (it *isn't* Fawlty Towers),
Black Friday Sales (when poets' visage sours):
'Blame these on men' some say. We're part in tune.

Songs and lyrics

How come no Guillotine
Sullied Britannia's scene?
Well, here's One Thing.
King George's Volunteers,
Well blest between the ears,
Lined up with Poets and Peers.
Long live the King.
Coleridge, Wordsworth, and Scott
Hardly smoked Rousseau's pot.
Burns joined the chain:
Volunteer Patriots,
Not 'useful idiots'
For Frenchy soviets.
Long may they Reign.

ii

Mrs Pankhurst:
Goodness me.
She turned Tory.
Let her be.
You can't fault her pedigree,
'Tricky' Mrs Pankhurst.

iii

We'll have to transgress the normative,
Eliminate the positive
And latch on to the conservative.

iv

The Brexit flag will do instead
While fraught Britannia's ill in bed.

v

What's-a matter you?
Hey! Gotta no respect.
You don' like my Brexit views.
Ah, shaddap-a you face!

vi

Thicko, Brexit thickos?
Guess what? I'm with thicko.
Guess what? I'm big at Kew.
Get this: I'm with thicko.
Guess why? He's no gnu.
(Apologies to Chumbawamba)

vii

Ignoramuses, that's what we is,
Ignoramuses, like Sir James Whiz.

viii

Sanctimonious, that's what you are,
And acrimonious in seminars.

ix

Intertextual, that's what you are,
And more susceptible in seminars.

x

The old home Trots look the same
As they come round once again,
And soon to meet them
There's old Paranoid and Drama.

xi

The avant-garde will do instead.
They'll show us how the World gets fed?

xii

Chomskis to the left of me,
Gramscis to the right. Here I stand.

xiii

They hate my dog as much as they hate kings.
I'd only named my King Charles Spaniel 'king'.
(Apologies to Cat Stevens)

xiv

Caitlin's Candy Mountain:
Oh, the Marxists and the fees
For their lucrative wheeze
'Round the soda water fountains
Whence their affluence springs
And the bluebird sings
In the Sunday Broadsheet Mountains.

xv

O Flower of Scotland
I'd fain not hear your words again.
There's some Scots loathed it,
'Your wee bit hill and glen'.
We wanted folk rock,
Steeleye and Fairport,
So headed southward
To turn again.

Sarcastic compliments sent in to the BBC

Dear BBC,

The News Quiz panellists put the puer back in puerile. Puer genius. Who would want them to mature. Will we ever, one wonders, have enough of it.

Yours truly,

Jonathan Swift

Dear BBC,

How nice it is to hear your news presenters defining student and anarchist protestors as 'people'. After all, in nature, and numerically, they are just like the rest of the public, quite typical.

Yours jointly:

Plato, Robert McKenzie, Peter Snow, Peter Kellner, and Tim Vine.

Dear BBC,

The scary anti-authority music and sound effects of your dark documentaries, dramas, and re-imaginings are spot-on, quite compelling, and only serve to underpin your objectivity and high standards. In fact, they state the case so well, might they not render the programme unnecessary? Just play the music and sound effects, or have the drama enhance them.

Yours,

Sir Simon Rattle.

Dear BBC,

It's good to see your news presenters indicating participant numbers for the enormous public demonstrations held in the UK capital in recent months. After all, who'd want to know about the turnout in comparison with electorate percentages, as you do with voters at a general election, especially when these unprecedentedly huge London demos actually attract a surprisingly small proportion of the electorate? Mind you, a comparatively small number of protestors actually feel the march is mightier than a general election turnout – or a high-turnout national referendum result. Plus big, colourful rallies in Trafalgar Square or Hyde Park with lots of noise, young, photogenic students, and children carrying parents' placards all make for good television. If only Glasgow or Edinburgh had a public park as big as

Hyde Park we would see that the SNP and Stop the War activists fill it to an eighth or more. You could, therefore, take an aerial shot of that. And the Edinburgh clip, of Princes Street Gardens and stage, might reveal more people shopping in Princes Street than at the Gardens protest.

Yours sincerely,

Edmund Burke.

Dear BBC,

Your bold follow-up programme to 'The Justifications of an Anti-Christ', 'The Memoirs of an Italian Anarchist', was inspired, and highly motivating. Are there more planned in this edgy arts series? I ask, as a fellow inmate has suggested this work, which he now has at hand: 'The Prison Notebooks of a Brummie Jihadi in Belmarsh Prison'.

Yours,

Otter, Inchoate Anarchist Federation.

… And the Great British Whinger? Don't get me started

* 'We are all Marxists now?'
  No. We are many whingers now. Those Marxist b******* have got us where they want us.

* Just because I'm suspicious doesn't mean to say they're not up to it.

* It's true you know. Political correctness is Socialism writ small. It is true.

* The London 2012 Whinging Olympic Games: the first gold medal for British whinging goes to … ?

* What's our favourite past-time?
  Britain onwhine.

* What's our commonest form of exercise?
  The British 4-minute whinathon.

* What's the gloomiest region in Britain?
  'Out There'. Postcode: UK.

* Come on, England. Why don't you tell us what you really think? Let rip and say, 'Damn, it's not on; no more Mr Nice Guy. That chancer Alex Salmond's not on, I tell you.'

* A definition of the impossible: a BBC TV programme entitled 'Whinging Britain'.

* What creature do you get if you cross BBC Radio 4 presenters John Humphrys and James Naughtie? One rude and sluggish Mega-Humpf: 'EVERYTHING IS BROKEN AND NOTHING'S FIT FOR PURPOSE! ... GOD, I WISH I WAS EXTINCT.'

* A cure for British whingers: citizens, consider your council wheelie bins, myriads of them, from Lerwick to Windsor, from Hackney to Binstead, Isle of Wight. Ignore the *Daily Mail*'s rubbishing of the service in parts of Leeds.

* Citizens, now allow your Inner Moaner to vent freely.

* Communists might, but disgruntled Britons won't wear a fascist frown.

Be bold

**Misery's our lot. Stand up. Perform with me
Two acts, both radical and alien:
Switch off the news, and, as it's so PC,
Renounce the Radio Times. Don't go arcadian.
More seismic still, give us good news, BBC.
Bestirred, we'd say it's too Orwellian.**

~~~~~~~~~~~~~~~

Glossary

Angry Brigade: on occasion used as a term for the left when seen as malcontents. Brigade members espoused revolutionary anarchist Communism, and carried out a series of small, publicity-grabbing bomb attacks in England between 1970 and 1972, including one on the Home Secretary. A BBC outside broadcast vehicle designated for coverage of the 1970 Miss World competition was another target. The Angry Brigade proved less deadly than the Baader-Meinhof Gang in Germany and the Red Brigade in Italy.

Anti-civ: short for 'anti-civilisation' anarchism.

Apologist: a category that includes those who hold to an ideological justification for murderous dictatorship or actions, or is a denier of such, eg, an apologist for Stalinist dictatorship or Pol Pot's 'Killing Fields'.

Bella Caledonia: a Scottish Nationalist (SNP) cultural website, its legend: Independence – Self-Determination – Autonomy. BC is based in Leith, Edinburgh; at mid-November, 2016, it had 7,156 subscribers to its blog. See **Scot Nat.**

Chumbawamba: 1986–2012; surely the best radical British alternative music band ever, and the most consistent.

Cloud-Cuckoo-Land: a realm of fantasy, dreams, or impractical notions; figures large in the lexicon for the left today, along with the expressions La La Land, moonbat, loony left, loony lefty, and MoneyTree. See **Moonbat** and **Socrates.**

Communism: a political movement based upon the writings of Karl Marx that divides society in accordance with economic categories and considers history interms of inevitable class conflict and revolutionary struggle. The words in the lexicon for Communists include: commie, a red, pinkoes, tankies, proles, Trots, Maoists.

CrimethInc: a purist and elitist Anarchist term, not easy to define in fewer than 400 words … and even then, I've tried, but lost the will to live. Not to be confused with Crimethink: the crime of having unorthodox or unofficial thoughts (thought crimes), mostly associated with Communist totalitarianism. The *Meditations* of Marcus Aurelius might be deemed a crimethink.

Critical Theory (CT): Marxist-derived theory that is critical of 'Capitalism', which it perceives as a system of domination and exploitation. The theory develops elaborate, emancipatory *critiques* of these. Initially, the term was used in the USA, by the Frankfurt School theorists, as a label to cover the Communist, anti-Capitalist content of their Marxism. Among its early influential cultural theorists was **Herbert Marcuse,** who had fled Nazi Germany in the mid-1930s along with the other Frankfurt theorists.They secured teaching positions at Columbia University, New York. **CT** is a key element in **Neo-Marxism.**

Cultural chutzpah: as much front as Tate Modern; an indispensable attribute in the Arts sector.

Cultural hegemony: the success of the 'dominant classes' in presenting their view of the world; the term derived from Marx's phrase 'dominant ideology'. See **Noam Chomsky.**

Cultural Marxism: see **Neo-Marxism.**

Deva Kumarasiri: Sri Lankan-born British citizen and ardent Anglophile; another Britophile is Gulam Noon, the UK 'Curry King' (1936–2015); from 1991–2009 Mr Kumarasiri was postmaster at Sneinton Boulevard, Nottingham. See **Terence Wright-Clod.**

Dialectical materialism: the economic, political, and philosophical system of Karl Marx and Friedrich Engels that combines traditional materialism and Hegelian dialectic.

Eejit or **eedjit:** see **Numpty.**

Frankie Boyle: let's shame his audience, rather; that's what's needed really.

Γινώσκω (Ancient Greek): **Ginōskō:** Come to know, perceive.

Hegemony: see **Cultural hegemony.**

Herbert Marcuse: see **Critical Theory.**

Hermeneutics: the study and interpretation of human behaviour and social institutions; discussion of the purpose of life.

Heterotopia (space): a concept of 'other spaces' created by **Michel Foucault;** an 'alternative' space in which one is freed from dominant (hegemonic) factors; in this sense, perceived as emancipatory, and a momentary 'utopia'. As part of his 'deconstruction' of conventional reality, Foucault's concept is the more demanding as he posits seven types of heterotopia.

Historicist/historicism (or historism): the term/s come under three fields of study – Sociological (Marx School), History/Historiographical (Old School), and Art & Architecture (Art School). The historist is concerned with establishing Historicity, that is, the historical actuality of persons and events in the past. The humanities, it seems, is now a foreign country or city – they do things divergently there. There is little go-between; it's a case of more betwixt.

Insurrecto: insurrectionary, insurgent, rebel.

Inveiglement: BBC lefty stand-up trickery.

Karl Marx (1818–1883): German founder of modern Communism. Marx lived in Britain from 1849. With Frederick Engels he wrote *The Communist Manifesto* (1848); his other major revolutionary work was *Das Kapital,* the first volume of which was published in 1867.

Marx was convinced that society was class-based and that middle-class domination would succumb to that of the working class. An 'urban explorer', Marx loved his regular 'strolls' on Hampstead Heath; there was nothing more liberating for him than this.

La La Land: an expression for a state of being that is out of touch with reality; largely reserved for the far left, often called the hard left. See **Cloud-Cuckoo -Land.**

Left: the supporters or advocates of varying degrees of social, political, or economic change, reform, or revolution.

Left-liberal intellectual: 'ethically aware', cerebral, pious, active, entitled, and demanding. Anandi's demanding PhD is entitled: 'The Liminality and Rhetoric of the Anti-Thatcherite Slogan: What Do We Want & When Do We Want It?! Now!' See **Liberal (a liberal).**

Leftist: tending towards or relating to the political left or its principles.

Left-wing: the leftist faction of an assembly, party, or group.

Lefty: a left-winger; one of the angry brigade.

Liberal (a liberal): a person who has liberal ideas or opinions; for adjectives applied, eg, **wishy-washy liberal,** see **Socialist.**

Michel Foucault (1926–1984): a French philosopher and social theorist of modernity. Foucault's theories of social control and power and how they are seen to operate through institutions are now well advanced in the mainstream. Foucault enthusiastically welcomed the Ayatollah-led Iranian Revolution of 1979, which sought to establish a Shiite Islamic Republic.

Militant Tendency: Masters of Trickery in the 1980s.

Momentum: Militant Tendency: Masters of Trickery in 2016. A leftie does not change its spots.

Moonbat: in the USA, a pejorative term referring to leftists, first used around 2006. The first word takes the meanings of lunar, unearthly, and perhaps lunacy, from which derived the English term 'loony'; to the latter would be added 'lefty' in 1987. Bat seems close to the British word 'batty', meaning demented or bonkers. See **Cloud-Cuckoo-Land.**

Neo-Marxism: often referred to as **Cultural Marxism,** the term is applied to any sociological analysis which draws on the ideas of Karl Marx and Friedrich Engels, but which amends or extends these by incorporating elements from other intellectual traditions, such as **Critical Theory,** psychoanalysis, existentialism, criminology, ethics, and human geography. There is no unified ideology of neo-Marxism in the way that there is in orthodox Marxism, and many of the former's currents are in fact not in agreement with one another.

Nicola, Ya Belter: a purely fictional song/title. In Scots slang, someone who is exceptional in some way might be addressed as 'you belter', or 'ya wee belter'.

Noam Chomsky (b. 1928): brought up within a broad Communist family group in Philadelphia, Chomsky has become the most influential of Marxist theorists today, with his theories of political **hegemony** in particular holding considerable sway on US and UK campuses, and among journalists, intelligentsia, and left-wing stand-up comedians. Marxist theories of **cultural hegemony** have their origins in the writings of Antonio Gramsci (1891–1937). Gramsci's theories of cultural dominance formed, in turn, the basis for **Cultural Marxism** in the later 20th century. Gramsci was founder member and leader of the Italian Communist Party (1921–1991).

Norm Gallagher (1931–2000): Federal Secretary of the Australian trade union, the Builders Labourers Federation. Born in the slums of Collingwood, Melbourne, the young Gallagher was a street fighter, tent boxer, and then builder's labourer. By the 1970 he was a prominent member of the Communist Party of Australia.

Numpty: in Scotland (and Lancashire), a pejorative word meaning a 'useless individual' or 'idiot' (eejit), sometimes uttered in respect of a politician or lone SWP or WRP protestor, rarely of Communist or Nazi **apologist** writers subsequently. Scots poet, or 'makar', Hugh MacDiarmid briefly warmed to Hitler during World War II; he was both a Communist and a **Scot Nat.** The word numpty has appeared a few times in the Scottish press, and in 2010 it was voted the favourite word among Scots.

NUS: National Union of Students, founded 1922; Neo-Uniformity Students, 2016.

Occupiers: their parents surely wouldn't put up with it at home.

Pirate Party: not fictional. Founded in 2006 in Sweden, Pirate parties support information privacy (though not for the state), freedom of information, open content on the web, reform of copyright and patent law, direct democracy, and civil rights. The PP logo is a black sail in full swell within a circle; other symbols are the skull and crossbones on black, and black with an orange diagonal. The Anarchist logo is a black flag aloft within a circle.

Plus ingenii quam sapientiae: more brains than sense, as my mother would have said.

Postmodernism: a multi-faceted theoretical approach which challenges the certainties and dualisms of modernism. It therefore promotes pluralism and difference. Others refute this, and have said it's a word that pretends to stand for an idea, and it would be nice to get rid of it. Postmodernism tended to begin by denying right and wrong or purpose, but always ended up by privileging Socialism.

Proletariat: in Marxist theory, the class of wage-earners, especially industrial workers, in a Capitalist society, whose only possession of significant material value is their labour.

Rocinante: Don Quixote's horse: his weary, idealistic, tilting double.

Scottish Jacobite Party: not a fiction. Founded in 2005, the SJP seeks the establishment of an independent Scottish republic in which the 'citizen' would be 'king'.

Scot Nat/Sottish National Party: social democrat; Centre-left; pro-European Union. Indyref: Scottish Independence Referendum, 2014.

Seamus Milne: you wouldn't know, would you. Has a lean and hungry look, and is quick to darken; an impoverished Scottish aristocrat perhaps; something of the night. On temporary mission from the *Guardian*, he is Jeremy Corbyn's Director of Strategy & Communications.

Sinn Fein (We Ourselves): democratic Socialist; left-wing Irish nationalism; pro-Syriza.

Situationist: someone who seeks to introduce 'new projects of resistance and transformation'; these are acts of dissent, typically: pranks, street art, graffiti slogans, and costume role-play (cosplay). Situationists espouse the theory that human behaviour is determined by surrounding circumstances rather than by personal qualities. Mark Thomas, the UK comedian and political satirist, is considered one, though he self-defines as a libertarian anarchist; it renders him a 'confused liberal'.

SlutWalk: a self-coined, radical feminist term naming a specific issue protest march (and 'worldwide movement'). The name arose, in 2011, as a direct response to a statement by a Toronto Police Services officer: 'Women should avoid dressing like sluts in order not to be victimized.' As such it is a protest against perceived 'victim-blaming'.

Snarky eg Anarchist: snide and sharply critical.

Socialism (a): in Marxist theory, a transitional stage in the development of a society from Capitalism to Communism, characterised by the distribution of income according to work rather than need.

Socialism singular (b): sic. See **Socialisms (c)**.

Socialisms plural (c): fragmentary; big on names:

In the UK: Communist Party of Britain (CP)
Communist Party of Britain (Marxist Leninist)
Communist Party of Britain (CPGB)
Left Alliance
New Communist Party of Great Britain
Revolutionary Communist Party of Great Britain
Socialist Party (Marxist Leninist)
Socialist Labour Party

Socialist Workers' Party
Workers' Revolutionary Party
Belfast Socialist Party
Scottish Socialist Party.

In the USA: Freedom Road Socialist Organization
Freedom Road Socialist Organization (there's two)
Socialist Party of America
Socialist Party of Missouri
Socialist Action
World Socialist Party of the United States
African People's Socialist Party
American Labour Party
American Workers Party
Democratic Socialists of America
New American Movement.

In New Zealand: Socialist Aotearoa
Beyond Resistance
Communist Workers' Group
Fightback
International Socialist Organization
Socialist Voice.

Socialism (d): inferior to Stoicism, rendering one Philosophical.

Socialist: phrases in the lefty lexicon include: wishy-washy socialist, bleeding-heart socialist, warm and fuzzy socialist, 'right-on', and angry brigade. These adjectives are sometimes applied to a liberal too, eg a wishy-washy liberal. See **Liberal (a liberal).** Will Self has called himself a wishy-washy socialist.

Socrates: the famous troublesome free-thinker was lampooned by the Greek playwright Aristophanes in his play *The Clouds*, first performed in 423 BC. Also sent-up were the unkempt students of the 'radical' Socrates; their university was mocked as the 'Thinkery'. See **Cloud-Cuckoo-Land.**

Solipsism: a theory in Anarchism, derived from philosophy, that your own existence is the only thing that is real or that can be known.

Stasi: Communist East Germany's highly effective secret police agency, especially active at the height of the Cold War (the subject hardly figures these days); formed 1950, dissolved 1990. The Stasi deeply penetrated East German society and showed the reliance of Communism on denunciations, surveillance, and terror. Family members were encouraged to spy on each other.

SWP: Socialists Worked-up Party.

Terence Wright-Clod, Lord Rush of Blighty: purely factual; inspired by the name of the *Viz* comic character Tarquin Wright-Pratt, reactive son of Malcolm and Cressida Wright-Pratt, new age 'ethically aware' middle-class parents. Blighty: British slang, used especially by troops serving abroad in World War I; meaning England, home; derived from the Hindi word *bilayati:* foreign land, England. See **Deva Kumarasiri.**

The Pub Landlord: yes, Al Murray gave up being an anti-UKIP/Pub Landlord comic persona and actually became a pub landlord. Perhaps deep down there was always a bit of the Pub Landlord in the astute Al Murray, and a bit of the patriotic anti-lefty. I've often wondered. If you love the Spitfire, well ...

To Tariq Ali@Verso Press/Bcc: these publishers are fictitious apart from the first four. Dave Spart (acus): a figure in *Private Eye* magazine who is a verbally incontinent left-wing agitator.

Trotskyite or **Trot:** someone who supports the theory of Communism formulated by the Russian revolutionary Leon Trotsky (1879–1940). To achieve Communism, Trotsky called for immediate worldwide revolution by the proletariat. Various conspiratorial communist groups arose from this eventually, including the Militant Tendency, which sought to hijack the British Labour Party, trade unions, and Liverpool City Council in the 1970s and early 1980s. Stalin had Trotsky murdered and Trotskyite groups were frequently attacked by official Communists.

Union of Soviet Socialist Republics (USSR):
Soviet Communism, 1922–1991
The Communist Party of Great Britain: 1920–1991
The Conservative Party (UK): 1834–present
The Labour Party: 1900/1906–1997–2015? 2016?
The Scottish National Party: 1934–present
The Church of England: 1534/1547–present
The Church of Scotland: 1560–present
The Royal National Lifeboat Institution: 1824–present
Dr Barnardo's Homes for Poor Children: 1866–present
Battersea Dogs & Cats Home:1860–present.

'Useful Idiots': a term possibly invented in Soviet Union to describe people, particularly Western leftist intellectuals, who blindly supported Lenin and Stalin while they were ordering countless atrocities. The term has been employed more recently to describe anti-NATO Scottish Nationalists and others.

Will Self (b. 1961): British novelist, self-identified wishy-washy Socialist, political commentator, and journalist. He has described himself as a psychogeographer and modern flaneur, that is, a 'stroller' or 'urban explorer'. In the 18th century the term was 'idler'. Dr Johnson wrote about them. The more privileged intelligentsia might be considered idlers, and the bohemian, and many a shifty anarchist. They have time on their hands.

WRP: Worst Revolutionary Proles.

Zapatistas: historically, followers of the Mexican revolutionary figure Emiliano Zapata (1879–1919). The militant **neo-Zapatistas** of the late 20th century drew on Zapata's brand of armed agrarian communalism, and added libertarian Marxism, anarcho- Communism, and radical democracy along with other elements. The enigmatic Subcomandante Marcos, the founder, in 1994, of the Zapatista Army of National Liberation, remains still the neo-Zapatista's masked spokesman, and a rebel icon popular with the world's leftist groups.

Lightning Source UK Ltd.
Milton Keynes UK
UKOW04f0612141217
314453UK00001B/362/P

9 781911 589228